For Mac

*"It is not down in any map;
true places never are."*

—Herman Melville,
Moby-Dick

VIKING
Penguin Young Readers Group
An imprint of Penguin Random House LLC
375 Hudson Street
New York, New York 10014

First published in the United States of America by Viking,
an imprint of Penguin Random House LLC, 2017

LIBRARY OF CONGRESS CATALOGING-IN-PUBLICATION DATA IS AVAILABLE
ISBN 9780670016532

Manufactured in China

1 3 5 7 9 10 8 6 4 2

THE QUEST FOR

The True Story of Explorer
Percy Fawcett and a Lost City
in the Amazon

GREG PIZZOLI

Viking

LESS THAN ONE hundred years ago, maps of the world still included large "blank spots": distant and dangerous lands that mapmakers and scientists had not yet explored. One of these blank spots was deep within the Amazon rain forest, in Brazil.

Legends told of an ancient city that had once thrived there and then been forgotten. But no one knew the exact location, or even if the city existed at all.

When British explorer Percy Fawcett heard these legends, he called the mythical city "Z." Maybe he chose this name because the lost city seemed to be the most remote place in the world, the final stop, like the last letter of the alphabet. He made finding Z his life's work.

Ever since he was young, Percy Fawcett had dreamed
of traveling the world and exploring new places.

He was born in 1867 in Devon, England. His father was
a fellow of the Royal Geographical Society, and his older
brother was a mountain climber and author of adventure
novels. Adventure ran in the Fawcett family blood.

Fawcett studied at the Royal Military Academy at Woolwich in London, and when he was nineteen he joined the British Royal Artillery, where he learned the art of gunnery—the use of large military weapons.

Fawcett left England to serve as an artillery officer at Fort Frederick, in present-day Sri Lanka. He served in the armed forces there for over a decade, but was bored by military life and spent his free time investigating the nearby jungles and waiting for the day when he could become a professional explorer.

Upon his return to England, Fawcett joined
the Royal Geographical Society in London.

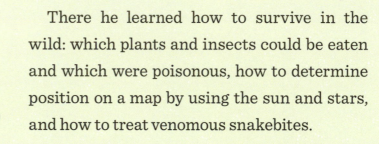

There he learned how to survive in the
wild: which plants and insects could be eaten
and which were poisonous, how to determine
position on a map by using the sun and stars,
and how to treat venomous snakebites.

After over a year of training at the RGS, he was ready for his first adventure.

I won't let you down, sir.

Just stay alive!

The president of the Royal Geographical Society hired Fawcett to lead an expedition into Bolivia, Brazil, and Peru. The RGS needed Fawcett to survey the borders of the three countries, which meant he had to go far into the jungle and carefully map everything he found.

THE ROYAL GEOGRAPHICAL SOCIETY

The Royal Geographical Society (RGS) is a research center and library dedicated to the study of geography and exploration. Since its founding in 1830, the RGS has been an important resource for scientists, explorers, and all people interested in mapmaking. Members of the RGS have included famed explorers Ernest Shackleton, Robert Falcon Scott, and Sir Edmund Hillary. The Royal Geographical Society is located in London. It regularly hosts exhibitions of historic photographs and artifacts from famous expeditions.

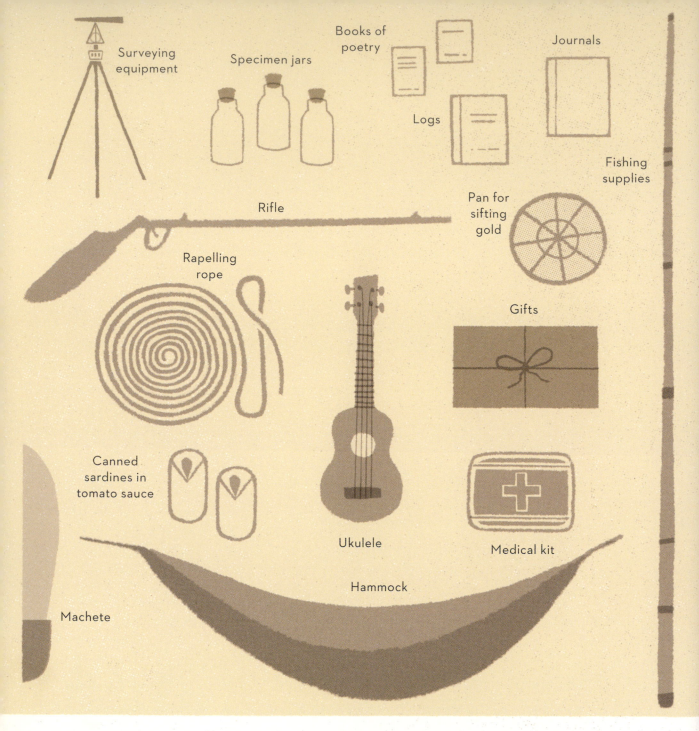

Surveying equipment

Specimen jars

Books of poetry

Logs

Journals

Fishing supplies

Rifle

Pan for sifting gold

Rapelling rope

Gifts

Canned sardines in tomato sauce

Ukulele

Medical kit

Machete

Hammock

Fawcett was thrilled to finally have the chance to do some real exploring, and excitedly prepared for the trip. He packed surveying instruments and logbooks, tools for climbing, a machete for hacking through the dense jungle, medical supplies, and gifts for any potentially hostile tribes he might encounter.

In May of 1906, he left his wife, Nina, and three year-old son, Jack, in England and sailed to South America.

PANAMA

VENEZUELA

COLOMBIA

THE GUIANAS

ATLANTIC OCEAN

ECUADOR

PERU

BRAZIL

Salvador

La Paz

BOLIVIA

PARAGUAY

CHILE

Asunción

ARGENTINE REPUBLIC

URUGUAY

PACIFIC OCEAN

Percy H. Fawcett Expedition Routes

1906 >>>>>>
1908 >>>>>>
1910 >>>>>>
1911 >>>>>>
1913 >>>>>>
1914 >>>>>>
1921 >>>>>>

This was just the first of many expeditions that Fawcett took to South America between 1906 and 1924.

On every trip, Fawcett and his different crews risked their lives in unforgiving landscapes in order to complete their surveying work. They mapped some of the most dangerous areas of the Amazon rain forest. Many in his company fell ill and even died in the wild—but no matter how serious the danger, Fawcett somehow always made it out alive. He thrived in the jungle.

He seemed almost unstoppable.

THE AMAZON RAIN FOREST

The Amazon is more than two million square miles of rain forest that extends into nine South American countries. Scientists estimate that there are as many as 16,000 different species of trees in the Amazon. The area is sometimes referred to as "the lungs of the world" because approximately 20 percent of Earth's oxygen is produced there. The Amazon contains millions of species of plants, insects, and birds, including many not yet known to science, and today new Amazon species are discovered at an average rate of one species every three days.

On one surveying expedition, Percy and his crew built canoes from fallen trees and set out down a tributary of the Amazon called the Rio Negro (Spanish for "Black River").

Percy and his men saw something near the water's edge, and as they got closer, it began to move toward them. Fawcett's crew panicked as they realized it was a giant anaconda!

Terrified at the thought of the snake's massive jaws—known to swallow pigs and caimans whole—Fawcett fired at the serpent with his rifle. When he was certain the snake was dead, he grabbed a specimen jar, hoping to slice off a bit of the anaconda's skin to take back to London.

He plunged his knife into its flesh, but the snake turned out to be very much still alive, and it attacked wildly. Fawcett's crew paddled away as fast as their oars would take them.

Later, the river grew very rough, so Fawcett and his men decided to carry their canoes through the forest to safer waters.

One of the crew went off from the group in search of a route through the jungle, but when he did not return, the rest went searching for him.

How long has he been gone?

Too long.

They found him half a mile inland,
dead, with forty-two arrows in his body.

On another journey, the RGS sent Fawcett to map hundreds of miles of jungle in northern Bolivia. Local officials warned Fawcett to stay away from a certain area of jungle because the natives who lived there would attack outsiders. Fawcett ignored these warnings. His mission from the RGS required him to scout the entire region and study its wildlife, and he was never one to turn away from danger.

One day while Fawcett's crew was canoeing in the dangerous area, poison-tipped arrows fell from the sky. This was the attack they had been warned about. They pulled the canoes to shore as they realized that they were surrounded.

As arrows fell around them, Fawcett gave a bizarre order: he told his crew to start singing. Fawcett and his men sang a medley of British songs together, accompanied by accordion, and the arrows stopped.

CROWNS AND THRONES MAY PERISH, KINGDOMS RISE AND WANE . . .

It was a risky move, but it worked,
and the two groups parted as friends.

Black Caiman

Annellated Coral Snake

Vampire Bat

As his primary mission was surveying, Fawcett kept extensive journals, logs, and drawings throughout all of his trips, which he later used to fortify his maps and reports to the RGS.

In addition to his field recordings, he wrote long accounts of the Amazon's living dangers, including poisonous spiders, giant anacondas, vampire bats, electric eels, and piranhas.

Candiru

Electric Eel

Piranha

Golden Poison Frog

Brazilian Wandering Spider

Perhaps most terrifying of all were the insects, which mercilessly attacked the explorers day and night. In addition to exhausting their victims through constant biting and stinging, the insects spread diseases which could be very painful and even fatal.

Burchell's Army Ant

Assassin Bug

Bullet Ant

Pium

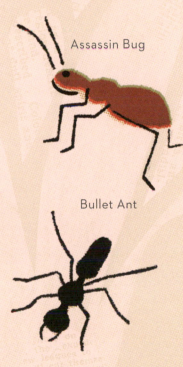

Green Anaconda

MOSQUITOES

In the United States, mosquitoes are usually seen by most people as nothing more than a nuisance, but mosquitoes are among the deadliest animals on Earth. There are over 3,500 species of mosquitoes in the world, and they are on every continent with the exception of Antarctica. Some of them spread diseases such as malaria, dengue fever, yellow fever, Zika, and West Nile virus, killing at least 750,000 people each year. By comparison, sharks are responsible for a grand total of 5 human deaths each year.

But simply surviving the horrors of the jungle was not enough for Percy Fawcett. He dreamed of completing an amazing quest that would secure his place in history.

On every trip to South America, Fawcett heard stories from locals that gave him clues to the possible location of the lost city of Z, and he became obsessed.

He imagined Z to be a large city built by an advanced civilization thousands of years ago. He pictured a paradise of grand temples and palaces carved from stone, hidden from modern man deep within the jungle.

Unfortunately for Fawcett, the experts at the Royal Geographical Society believed that the Amazon rain forest could never have supported such a city, and the legend of Z was simply a myth.

But that didn't stop Fawcett. He knew that the discovery of Z would be the adventure of a lifetime, make him rich and famous, and ensure that he would go down in history as one of the world's greatest explorers. All he had to do was find it.

FAMOUS EXPLORERS

Percy Fawcett lived at a time when explorers were celebrities. People all over the world breathlessly read accounts of their new discoveries. Fawcett's quest for Z must have been inspired in part by the success and failures of so many other explorers around the world.

In 1911, Hiram Bingham brought to the world stage the city of Machu Picchu, built by the Incas in the fifteenth century in what is now Peru, after local guides showed him the exact location. He wrote a book describing the rediscovery and later became an American senator.

After serving two terms as President of the United States of America, Theodore Roosevelt traveled to the Amazon with Brazilian explorer Cândido Rondon, and in 1913 explored the thousand-mile "River of Doubt." The river was later renamed Rio Roosevelt in his honor.

Years passed, and Fawcett carefully planned his expedition to find Z.

$$\left(\frac{\text{(ATLANTIS?)}}{5\sqrt{\ }}\right) \times \dots = Z$$

He would bring only a skeleton crew of people he knew he could trust: his son Jack, now twenty-one, and Jack's childhood friend Raleigh Rimell, who had both grown up hearing the amazing stories of Fawcett's previous adventures.

Without the full support of the RGS, Fawcett had to sell his story to newspapers, agreeing to let them write about every step of his expedition in exchange for the cash he needed to pay for the trip.

But what if you don't find anything, Lieutenant Fawcett?

It's **Colonel** Fawcett, thank you.

They worked out a system of "runners"—locals who would carry Percy Fawcett's handwritten reports out of the jungle—so that the newspapers could publish the story of the hunt for Z as it happened.

In April of 1925, Percy, Jack, and Raleigh set out into the jungle of Brazil, bringing with them two dogs, four horses, eight donkeys to carry supplies, and two local men to act as guides for the first part of the journey.

For the first month of the expedition, Fawcett sent letters back home through the runners, and newspapers printed reports of the explorers' progress across perilous landscapes, making their way toward the unexplored jungle.

The stories catapulted Percy Fawcett to international celebrity stardom, and readers around the globe waited eagerly for news of the discovery of Z.

One month into their journey, after crossing the Rio das Mortes ("River of Death") Percy, Jack, and Raleigh wrote the last of the letters that were carried out by their two guides.

Then the three explorers set off alone into the unexplored jungles of Brazil.

We do not need luck. It is my destiny.

Good luck, Fawcett.

I expect to be in touch with the old civilization within a month and to be at the main objective in August.

Thereafter our fate is in the lap of the gods.

PHFawcett

They were never seen again.

At first, people were not that concerned, because they assumed the Fawcett party would soon send news.

The world held out hope for the explorers' triumphant return and the discovery of Z.

Joan Fawcett, daughter

Nina Fawcett, wife

Brian Fawcett, younger son

But as time passed, a happy ending seemed less and less likely. Many hoped the explorers were still alive, but feared they had been taken captive, or were so weakened by the trip that they were unable to return without rescue. Newspapers were filled with rumors about what might have happened to them.

After a few years, most people accepted that they would never solve the mystery of how the quest for Z had ended. It seemed the unstoppable Percy Fawcett had been stopped at last.

But for some, the fascination over "The Lost City of Z" and the Fawcett party didn't end with their disappearance. In the nearly one hundred years since Percy, Jack, and Raleigh went missing, treasure hunters, fame-seekers, and even movie stars have gone into the jungle to find out what happened to Percy Fawcett. None have been successful.

It's estimated that as many as one hundred people have disappeared or died in the hunt for Percy Fawcett and the blank spot on the globe that he called Z.

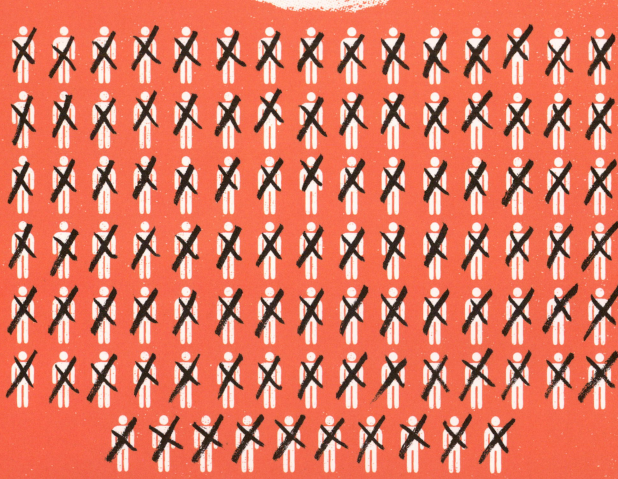

Almost a century after Percy Fawcett's final expedition, archeologists and researchers found conclusive evidence proving there were in fact ancient cities in the Amazon. By using modern technology that Percy Fawcett could never have imagined—such as satellite photos and radar imaging—scientists have found artifacts from human settlements in the Amazon as far back as ten thousand years. And as early as AD 800–1600, people living in the very area where Fawcett thought he would find Z had made pottery, built roads, and even designed bridges!

Although these settlements do not resemble the grand stone palaces that Fawcett expected to find, his belief that large cities in the Amazon existed has finally been proven correct. We may never know if Fawcett saw these cities for himself, but we do know that they were out there.

Fawcett became famous, just as he always wanted—but ironically, it was not for his success as an explorer but for his failure. Although it wasn't the way he'd imagined it, his amazing adventures and his unparalleled passion for finding the city he called Z have granted him a place in history. As for what happened to Percy Fawcett, Jack Fawcett, and Raleigh Rimell—it's still a mystery.

Author's Note

THERE WERE A FEW TIMES while working on this book that I myself felt I had lost my way. Telling Fawcett's story was difficult at times, because he was not a typical hero. He had a frenzied belief that the world was wrong, that he was right, and that he alone could prove it. And in many ways, his life was marked by failure.

For me, this story came together in Central America. I took a vacation there with my family to bask in the warm sun while my home in Philadelphia suffered a particularly cold winter. About a week into our trip, my brother-in-law and I were visiting a jaguar preserve in Belize, and we jumped out of our jeep to see what a sign called "Plane Wreck Trail." It couldn't have been more than a tenth of a mile off the main road, but all the same I got chills as we walked through the jungle at dusk, with jaguars supposedly around and the constant hum of mosquitos attacking us. In a clearing at the end of the trail was a small plane, which had crashed there decades ago. Huge plants taller than houses surrounded it, and I began to understand how frightening the jungle can be, how alone one can feel, how perilous every step could seem.

On that same trip, we also traveled to the ruins of Tikal, in Guatemala. Seeing the great pyramids emerge from the jungle, I felt overcome by how old the world is, how much there is to see, and how many people have come before us. And I felt bad for Fawcett. He never saw Z like this.

The search for truth is something that simmers inside all of us. We all hunt for unknowable answers, and dream of places where the problems of our lives will dissolve away. We know now that Fawcett was partly right about Z, but I think it's safe to assume that after a lifetime of searching, Fawcett felt he had failed. He never returned home with the proof he needed to convince the rest of world.

Personally, I don't believe that Fawcett wanted to find Z solely because it would be an important geographic discovery, or because it would make him famous, rich, and respected. Finding Z would have given his life purpose. If the final path led to Z, it was all worth it. In the end, he risked everything to discover the unknown. In his own words, he "chose the forest path," and he got lost. He went off the map.

FAWCETT HUNTERS

George Dyott: In 1928, British aviator and explorer George Dyott led a large expedition in search of Percy Fawcett. While in Brazil, he spoke with members of the Kalapalo tribe, who told him that a neighboring tribe had murdered Percy, Jack, and Raleigh. Dyott wrote a book about his experience called *Man Hunting in the Jungle: The Search for Colonel Fawcett*, and later starred in a film adaptation called *Savage Gold*.

Albert de Winton: In 1934, Hollywood actor Albert de Winton made a well-publicized trip to Brazil in search of Fawcett, but soon ran into trouble. A note from de Winton emerged from the jungle, saying that he was being held against his will by a local tribe. He asked the Brazilian government for help, but they refused, and he was never seen again.

The Villas Bôas brothers: In 1952, members of the Kalapalo tribe told the explorers Cláudio, Leonardo, and Orlando Villas Bôas that some of their own had killed the Fawcett party. They even supplied a skeleton as proof. However, the bones were examined by the Royal Anthropological Society in London, who determined they belonged to a man no taller than 5'7", and therefore could not have belonged to Percy Fawcett, who was nearly 6'2". Apparently the tribe had invented the story and sent the bones of a Kalapalo man, perhaps to scare off any more potential Fawcett-hunters from intruding on their land.

Father and son: In 1996, James Lynch, a millionaire from Brazil, financed an expedition to discover what happened to Fawcett. He brought along his sixteen-year-old son as well as GPS, radio, and every gadget a modern team traveling the Amazon could hope for. However, as they approached Fawcett's last known whereabouts, the Lynch team was held captive by tribesmen and were only released after they gave up about $30,000 worth of equipment to their captors.

Glossary

Ancient: from a time in the distant past.

Artillery: the branch of the armed forces that designs and uses mounted guns for use in warfare.

Caiman: a large, semiaquatic reptile related to the crocodile and alligator, found in Central and South America.

Civilization: a culture or society of people from any specific time or place.

Expedition: a journey taken by a group of people with a shared goal.

Fellow: a member of a society formed by like-minded people.

Geography: the study of the physical features of the earth including climate, natural landforms such as mountains and rivers, plant and animal distribution, as well as the way those physical features affect the aspects of human culture such as the building of cities, language, and religion.

Machete: a large, heavy knife, used for cutting through plants and as a weapon.

Mythical: imaginary, not supported by direct evidence or fact.

Quest: a long search made in order to find something meaningful.

Rain forest: a dense forest rich in plant and animal life, in an area with regularly heavy rainfall.

Remote: far away, located in a place with little else around.

Surveying: the science related to determining the exact form and boundaries of a section of land such as a country or town, for political or scientific use.

Tributary: a river or stream that flows into a larger body of water.

Selected Sources

Books

Childress, David Hatcher. *Lost Cities & Ancient Mysteries of South America*. Stelle, Ill.: Adventures Unlimited Press, 1986.

Churchward, Robert. Illustrated by Robert Hodgson. *Explorer Lost!: The Story of Colonel Fawcett*. Edinburgh: Thomas Nelson and Sons, 1957.

Fawcett, Percy H. *Exploration Fawcett*. London: Century, 1988.

———. Edited by Brian Fawcett. *Lost Trails, Lost Cities*. New York: Funk & Wagnalls, 1953.

Fleming, Peter. *Brazilian Adventure*. New York: C. Scribner's Sons, 1934.

Grann, David. *The Lost City of Z: A Tale of Deadly Obsession in the Amazon*. New York: Doubleday, 2009.

Wallace, Scott. *The Unconquered: In Search of the Amazon's Last Uncontacted Tribes*. New York: Crown, 2011.

Newspaper Articles

"Angeleno Goes with Explorer." *Los Angeles Times,* Jan. 15, 1925.

"Bugs in Attack on Explorers." *Los Angeles Times*, Dec. 3, 1925.

"Colonel Fawcett—The Great Riddle of the Jungle." *The Sunday Herald,* May 3, 1953.

"Expedition May Startle World." *Los Angeles Times,* Apr. 16, 1925.

"Explorers Enter Jungles to Seek Lost White Race." *Los Angeles Times*, Dec. 1, 1925.

"Meeting Place of Human Tide." *Los Angeles Times,* Apr. 21, 1925.

"Party Enters Brazil Jungle." *Los Angeles Times,* Apr. 23, 1925.

"Search On for Missing Explorers." *Los Angeles Times,* July 10, 1927.

"Unique Outfit for Explorer." *Los Angeles Times,* Jan. 13, 1925.

"Wager Lives on Old Adage." *Los Angeles Times*, Dec. 2, 1925.

Websites

Grann, David. "The Lost City of Z: A Quest to Uncover the Secrets of the Amazon." *The New Yorker*, September 19, 2005. http://www.newyorker.com/magazine/2005/09/19/the-lost-city-of-z.

History. *History in the Headlines*. http://www.history.com/news/explorer-percy-fawcett-disappears-in-the-amazon-90-years-ago.

History. *History Lists*. http://www.history.com/news/history-lists/6-explorers-who-disappeared.

NOTE: The lyrics sung by Fawcett and companions on p. 21 are from the folk song "Onward Christian Soldiers," which Fawcett noted in his memoirs that they sang during the incident.

ACKNOWLEDGMENTS

I'd like to offer my sincere thanks to Leila Sales, Joanna Cárdenas, Jim Hoover, Denise Cronin, Ken Wright, Janet Pascal, Steven Malk, Rotem Moscovich, Mac Barnett, and as always, my wife, Kay. Another book that wouldn't exist without your generosity. Thank you.

I'd also like to thank the staff of the Royal Geographical Society Foyle Reading Room—most especially Jan Turner, who was very helpful in finding the documents from their collection that helped me design the pictures for this book.

ART NOTE

The art in this book was made using silkscreen, photographic halftones, Zipatone, photocopy machines, newspapers, cut paper, and Photoshop. Inspiration for much of the art came from photographs and drawings made by the author during trips to Central America and Southeast Asia.